Table of Contents

Where To?

People travel all over town. They travel to school, work, and the store. They travel to many other places, too. People use maps to get where they are going.

Maps help people know where to drive.

Map Maker

A cartographer (kahr-TOG-ruh-fur) is a person who makes maps.

This cartographer is making a map.

Give Me Directions!

Maps have a **compass rose**. This is a design that shows directions. The directions are *north*, *south*, *east*, and *west*. A map might show you that your school is east of your house.

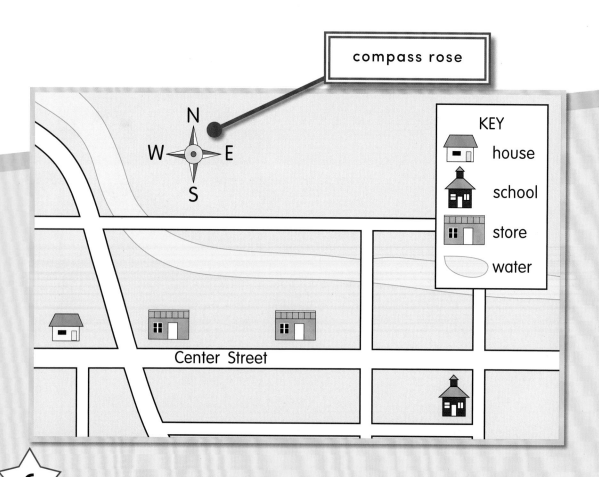

compass rose

KEY

house

school

store

water

Center Street

Two friends look at a map in a city.

Using Maps

A town map is a picture of a whole town. The **key** tells you what the lines, shapes, and colors mean. Each **symbol** (SIM-buhl) shows a place in town.

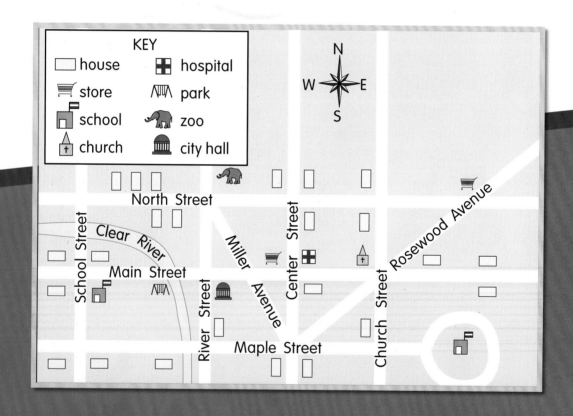

This map has a key at the top.

A Map of the Stars

Long ago, people used the stars as a map. The star patterns helped them find their way.

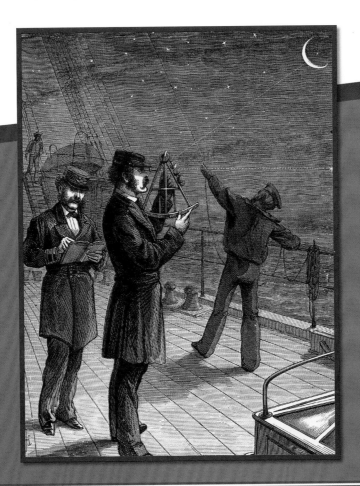

A sailor finds his way by looking at the stars.

The lines on a map show roads, from large highways to small streets. People use these roads to get from place to place. Blue lines and shapes on maps show areas of water.

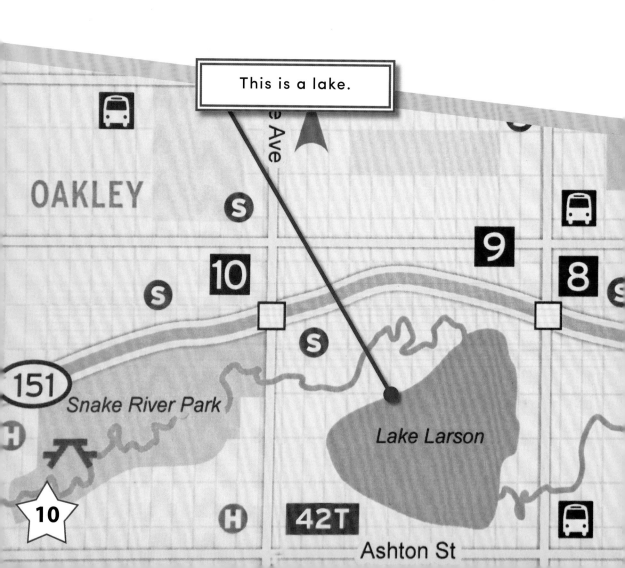

This is a lake.

OAKLEY

151

Snake River Park

Lake Larson

42T

Ashton St

10

Important Places

Map symbols show important places. A bus may show a bus stop. A table may show a picnic area.

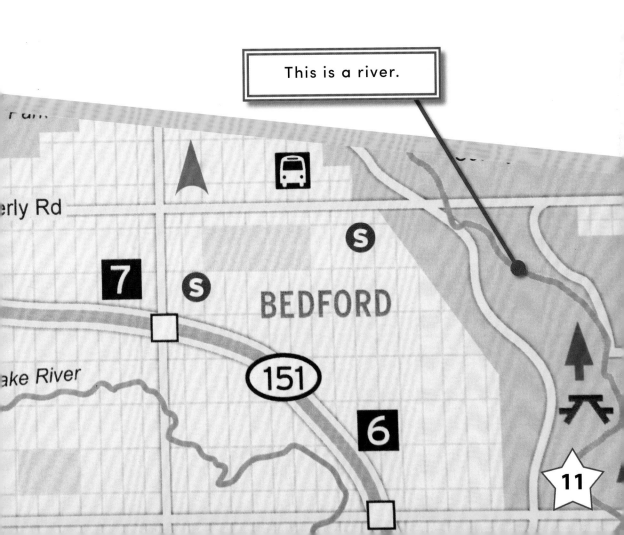

This is a river.

erly Rd

BEDFORD

7

151

ake River

6

How Far?

Real places and the **distance** between them are drawn much smaller on maps than they really are. A map's **scale** tells you how to measure distances on the map. One inch may **equal** (EE-kwuhl) one mile.

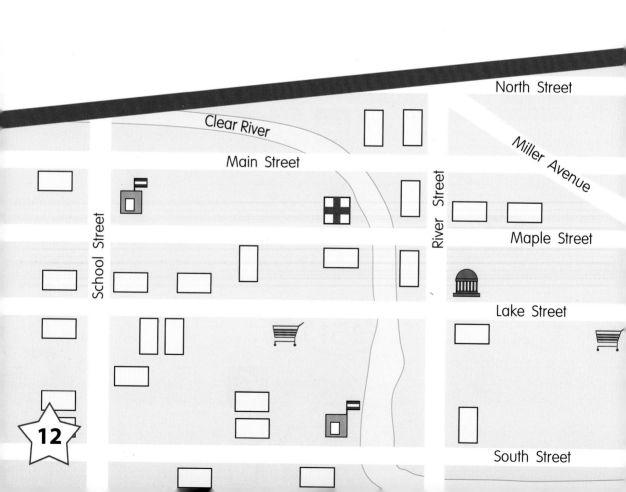

Large Scale

On a map of the world, one inch can equal 1,000 miles!

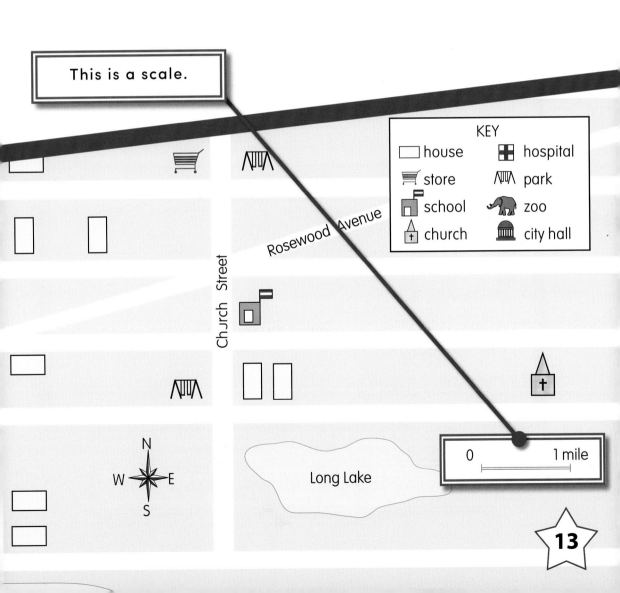

This is a scale.

KEY

☐ house		✚	hospital
🛒 store		⋔	park
🏫 school		🐘	zoo
⛪ church		🏛	city hall

Rosewood Avenue

Church Street

Long Lake

0   1 mile

N
W · E
S

On the Grid

A map may be drawn on a **grid** with lines. A grid has letters or numbers along two sides. There is a rectangle where each letter and number meet. You can find a place by looking for its rectangle.

	A	B	C	D
1	Main Street		Miller Avenue	
2			Maple Street	
3		River Street	Lake Street	Center Street
4			Long Lake / South Street	

This map has a grid. It shows a house in C3.

14

Computer Maps

Many people use computers for maps. The computer helps them know where to go.

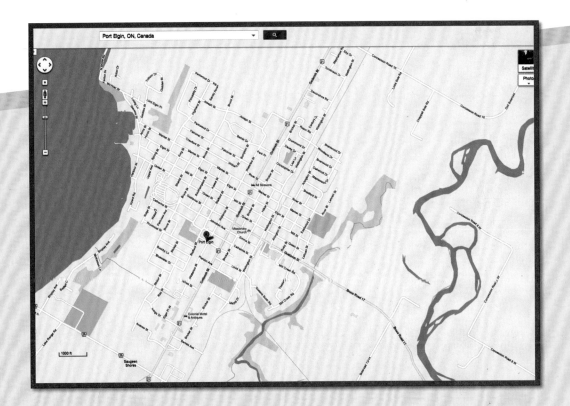

This map is from a computer.

Which Way?

Maps help people give directions. Maps can help you decide whether you should go north, south, east, or west. You will know where to turn and how far to travel.

This invitation has a map.

This boy shows his grandpa a place on a map.

Become a Map Master!

All towns are different. But every town has a map. The parts of the map will help you know where you are. Learn how to read maps so you can get around any town!

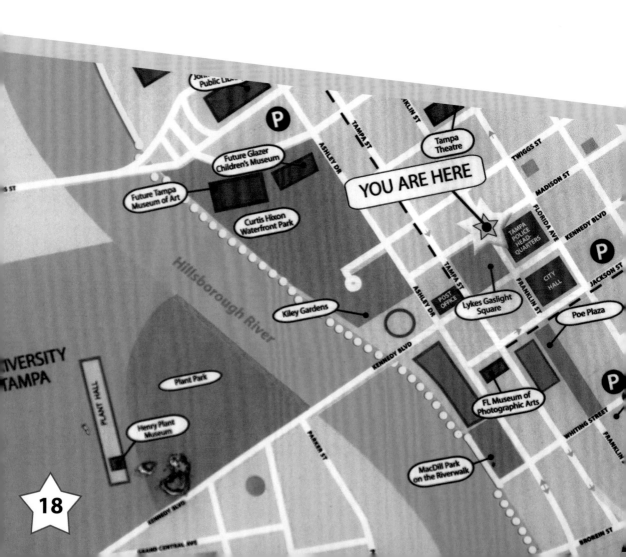

A girl and her dad use a map on their trip.

Map It!

Draw a map of your town. Include the places below. Add a compass rose and a key, too. Then tell a friend how to get from your house to a place in town.

Places

city hall	my school
fire station	park
hospital	police station
library	post office
my house	supermarket

This boy draws a map of his town.

Glossary

compass rose—a design on a map that shows north, south, east, and west

distance—the amount of space between two places

equal—the same

grid—a pattern of lines that cross each other to form rectangles

key—a list that tells what the symbols on a map mean

scale—a line used to measure distances on a map

symbol—a picture or a shape on a map that stands for a real place or thing

Index

Your Turn!

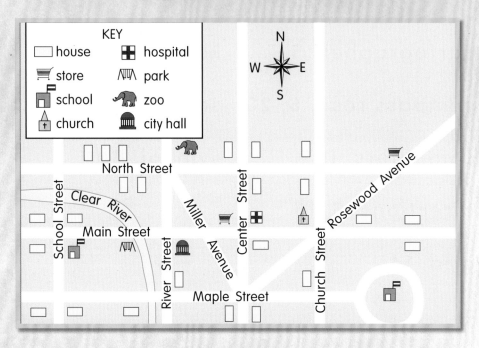

Can You Find It?

This map shows many places. It has a key to help you. Can you find a store? Can you find a school? How did you find those places?